HOW TO PLAY THE BASS

A Beginner's Guide to Learning the Basics of the Bass, Reading Music, and Playing Songs with Audio Recordings

Legal & Disclaimer

The information contained in this book and its contents is not designed to replace or take the place of any form of medical or professional advice; and is not meant to replace the need for independent medical, financial, legal or other professional advice or services, as may be required. The content and information in this book has been provided for educational and entertainment purposes only.

The content and information contained in this book has been compiled from sources deemed reliable, and it is accurate to the best of the Author's knowledge, information, and belief. However, the Author cannot guarantee its accuracy and validity and cannot be held liable for any errors and/or omissions. Further, changes are periodically made to this book as and when needed. Where appropriate and/or necessary, you must consult a professional (including but not limited to your doctor, attorney, financial advisor or such other professional advisor) before using any of the suggested remedies, techniques, or information in this book.

Upon using the contents and information contained in this book, you agree to hold harmless the Author from and against any damages, costs, and expenses, including any legal fees potentially resulting from the application of any of the information provided by this book. This disclaimer applies to any loss, damages or injury caused by the use and application, whether directly or indirectly, of any advice or information presented, whether for breach of contract, tort, negligence, personal injury, criminal intent, or under any other cause of action.

You agree to accept all risks of using the information presented in this book.

You agree that by continuing to read this book, where appropriate and/or necessary, you shall consult a professional (including but not limited to your doctor, attorney, or financial advisor or such other advisor as needed) before using any of the suggested remedies, techniques, or information in this book.

Table of Contents

Throughout this book there are musical examples and audio recordings to follow along with on your journey to learn how to play the clarinet.

Whenever you see the following text:

AUDIO EXAMPLE Track #

Please follow along with the recordings at the Sound Cloud link below or search on Sound Cloud for "How to Play the Bass".

https://soundcloud.com/jason_randall/sets/how-to-play-the-bass

It is recommended to bookmark this page.

Chapter 1
Introduction

If you are reading this, you have decided you want to learn how to play the bass guitar. While it is often overlooked in comparison to its flashier sibling, the acoustic/electric guitar, bass guitar is the backbone of any musical ensemble. As the essential link between rhythm, melody, and harmony, it is the glue that holds bands together and the foundation upon which most popular music styles are built. This book will teach you everything you need to know to build a solid foundation and begin your musical journey.

A Brief History of the Bass Guitar

The origins of what is now known as the electric bass guitar can be traced all the way back to an instrument called the **viola da gamba,** or **viol** for short. This instrument first appeared in Spain during the 15th century, was played with a bow or sometimes plucked, and typically had five to seven strings and several **frets** made of animal gut (you read that correctly) for consistency of intonation.

The next branch on the evolutionary bass tree is an instrument known as the **double bass**. A member of the violin family, it can also be called the **contrabass,** which is a term for the musical range it occupies - one **octave** below the 'bass' register (the range of a cello). As you will see, there are all kinds of names for this instrument.

A viola da gamba in its silky habitat

The **double bass** is the largest and lowest-pitched instrument in the modern symphony orchestra and like the **viol**, it is played with a bow and sometimes plucked (a technique called pizzicato). Unlike its Spanish ancestor, the **double bass** is fretless, just like the violin, so players must pay careful attention to precise finger position to play 'in-tune.' Another way the **double bass** differs from the **viol** is in the number of strings. For most of its history, the **double bass** had only 3 strings, picking up a 4th sometime around the turn of the 20th century.

The classical orchestra wasn't the only place where the **double bass** found a home. By the 1920s, jazz groups in New Orleans had shifted from marching in the streets to performing inside clubs, bars, and brothels. The **double bass,** or **upright bass** as they preferred to call it, became the instrument of choice for bass players, replacing the tubas and sousaphones used by marching bands.

To keep up with the sheer volume of the horn sections in these bands, and since amplification did not exist at this time, bass players developed a slap-style of striking the strings. This technique involved both slapping the strings with the plucking hand and pulling the strings perpendicular to the fretboard, causing them to rebound against it. This created a more percussive sound that could punch through and be heard alongside the louder instruments.

The double bass or upright bass

Initially, early jazz bassists mimicked the 'two-beat' feel or 'boom-chick' rhythm that was previously played by the tuba and can still be heard as an accompaniment style in folk, country, bluegrass, rockabilly, and a slew of other genres originating in the United States. Soon enough, **stand-up bass** (yet another synonym for the **double bass**) players were using what is now called 'walking bass' style to accompany tunes. **Wellman Braud**, who began his career in New Orleans and eventually found his way into the world-famous **Duke Ellington** orchestra, is credited with introducing this style, which has since become a mainstay of jazz and blues.

The **upright bass** has a rich history in western music and is still the primary bass register instrument in classical, jazz, rockabilly, psychobilly, bluegrass, folk, and other traditional genres. In the 1930s, **Paul Tutmarc**, a Seattle area singer, multi-instrumentalist, and inventor, singlehandedly revolutionized the bass world when he created the first **electric bass guitar**. In 1935, his company, *Audiovox*, began producing the 'Model 736 Bass Fiddle,' a solid-bodied instrument with 4 strings and 16 steel frets. This instrument was compact and easy to carry, electronically amplified, and designed to be played in a horizontal position (as opposed to the vertical playing position of the upright bass). Only about 100 of these instruments were made. They were not adopted by players on a grand scale, but they were a huge step toward the developments that lay around the corner.

Paul Tutmarc posing with his creations, including the 'Model 736 Bass Fiddle (middle)

In 1950, Leo Fender and George Fullerton of *Fender Electric Instrument Manufacturing Company,* or *Fender* for short, created the world's first mass-produced **electric bass guitar**, the Precision Bass or 'P-Bass.' With its ergonomic, light-weight, contoured body design, the Fender P-Bass offered working musicians a much more practical and portable instrument than the amplified double bass, which was large and cumbersome, and often generated unwanted feedback, which the solid construction of the *P-Bass* mitigated. **Monk Montgomery**, brother of legendary guitarist Wes Montgomery, was one of the first musicians to adopt the *P-Bass* as his main touring instrument. Others soon followed, including Elvis Presley's bassist

Bill Black, who got rid of his upright bass for good in 1957. Another advantage of the *P-Bass* was its similarity to the electric guitar, which made it easy for guitarists to play.

The legendary 1952 Precision Bass by Fender

As they say, "competition breeds innovation" and the *Gibson Guitar Corporation* showed that the reverse was also true when they introduced a violin-shaped 4-string electric instrument which eventually came to be known as the EB-1 in 1953 (E for electric and B for bass if you didn't put that together). Soon enough, all kinds of electric bass guitars were being manufactured by companies like *Rickenbacker, Danelectro, Kay,* and *Höfner,* whose now famous *500/1* model eventually found its way into the capable hands of Paul McCartney of a little group called The Beatles.

The legendary 500/1 violin bass by Höfner. Often called the "Beatle bass" due to its association with Paul McCartney.

By the 1960s, Detroit-based label *Motown Record Corporation* was dominating the charts with hit after hit by superstars like the Marvellettes, the Supremes, the Temptations, Marvin Gaye, the Four Tops, Little Stevie Wonder, and countless others. At the center of the Motown hit machine were the Funk Brothers, a group of session musicians who provided the music for almost all the label's recordings from 1959 to 1972. Legendary bassist **James Jamerson** was responsible for some of the Funk Brothers' most memorable bass lines of the time. His P-Bass can be heard all over hits like "Ain't No Mountain High Enough," "My Girl," "I Was Made To Love Her," "I Heard It Through The Grapevine," and many more. His style went on to influence a generation of electric bass players in a myriad of genres and he is considered to be one of the greatest electric bassists of all time.

James Jamerson digs into his P-Bass at Motown Studios.

On the west coast of America in Los Angeles, a group of studio musicians known as the Wrecking Crew were also laying down a formidable catalogue of chart-topping hits. Credited with creating the 'wall of sound' recording technique alongside producer Phil Spector, the Wrecking Crew provided the music for many popular films and television programs, as well as artists like Frank Sinatra, Sonny & Cher, The Mamas and the Papas, and the Beach Boys, and also acted as 'ghost band' for groups like The Byrds, The Monkees, and maybe even a few Bob Dylan tracks. Holding down the low end in the Wrecking Crew was **Carol Kaye**, who started out as a 6-string guitarist and continued using a pick to pluck the strings once she switched over to bass and created her signature sound. She is often credited as the 'most prolific bass player of all time,' having appeared on over 10,000 recordings in her career, many of which were hits.

When the British Invasion hit in the mid-sixties, Paul McCartney was instrumental in taking the bass guitar out of the shadows and putting it front and center in the eyes of millions of rock fans. His melodic, catchy basslines were a key part of what made the Beatles so successful, and other bands like the Rolling Stones, the Kinks, and the Who further helped to propagate the role of bass in popular music. The Who's **John Entwistle** stands out as a true innovator of the rock bass sound, using stereo amplification to send out both *distorted* high-end frequencies and *clean* low-end frequencies. He also pioneered a rapid-fire plucking technique known as the 'typewriter' that matched perfectly with the machine gun rhythms of guitarist Pete Townsend and went on to influence many bassists on the heavier, flashier side of rock music, like Billy Sheehan, David Lee Roth, Steve Vai, and Chris Squire.

While all of this was going on, James Brown was touring and performing relentlessly, fusing soul and r & b to create a genre of music that came to be known as funk. His band The James Brown Band, or the JBs as they were known in the 70s, was a veritable finishing school for masters of groove. Bassists like Fred Thomas, Bernard Odum, and most famously Bootsy Collins laid down steady, booty-shaking basslines that provided the foundation on which funk was built. Their grooves gained a second life, as they are ubiquitous in hip hop, which relies heavily on samples. Who is the most sampled artist of all time? James Brown of course.

No talk of funk bass is complete without mentioning the legendary **Larry Graham** whose tenure with Sly and the Family Stone and Graham Central Station produced a slew of hits. He is credited with pioneering the *slap and pop* technique, a highly percussive style of playing that emulates the sound of a kick drum and snare with the plucking hand thumb and finger, respectively. This style was a huge innovation in expanding the sonic capabilities of the bass and an influence on other legendary players like Flea of the Red Hot Chili Peppers, Les Claypool of Primus, Victor Wooten, and many more.

With the arrival of the early 70s, electric bass took another leap forward and hybridized with its fretless ancestor the **double bass**. In an effort to sound more like the acoustic stand-up bass used extensively in jazz, virtuoso fusion bassist **Jaco Pastorius** ripped the frets off his Fender J-Bass and carved out a rightful place for the bass guitar as a lead improvisational instrument.

A fretless Fender Jazz Bass as played by Jaco Pastorius

Today, bass is everywhere, and although newer instruments like synthesizers and software instruments may be finding their way into popular music, the human touch and warm tone of the electric bass is still a hot commodity. Hopefully you can now appreciate how far the bass guitar has come to get into your hands. With all the resources available at your fingertips, there has never been a better time to learn. Let's get to it!

Chapter 2
Bass Anatomy 101

Topics covered:

- Parts of the bass and what they look like

- How basses work

- Tuning your bass

Can't tell your headstock from your lower bout? Wondering what all those knobs and switches do? Want to tune your bass but can't figure out what pegs to turn? This chapter will help you learn the parts of the bass guitar, what they do, and what they look like.

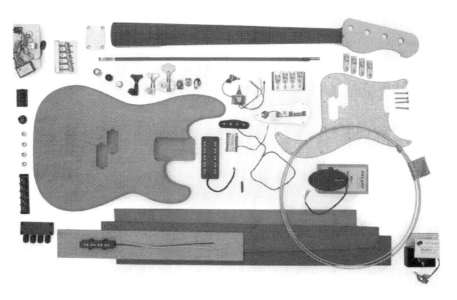

Parts of the Bass

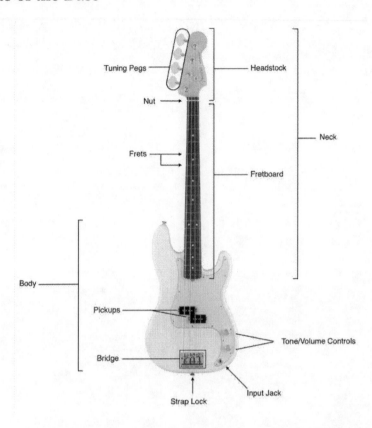

Body: This is the largest section of the bass and is responsible for the resonance and overall tone of the instrument. Depending on the type of guitar, bodies are either *solid, hollow*, or *semi-hollow*. Bass guitar bodies come in all shapes and sizes and are mostly made of wood, but also come in aluminum, plastic, and even cardboard. Being the largest part of the guitar, the body contains many smaller parts including the bridge, pickguard, volume pots, pickups, and input jack.

Bridge: Located on the lower bout (lower half) of the bass guitar body, the bridge acts as an anchor for the strings. It is typically made of metal.

Cutaway: An indent or two (single vs. double cutaway) in the upper bout of the guitar designed to grant easier access to the higher frets.

Frets: The metal wires that lie on the fretboard, perpendicular to the strings. When the string is depressed behind the fret, the length is effectively shortened and a unique pitch is produced. The closer to the bridge you get, the higher the fret number, the shorter the string length, and therefore the higher the pitch (and vice versa).

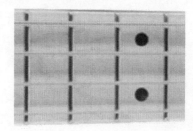

Fretboard: A plank of wood attached to the neck in which the *frets* are embedded. This is also called the *fingerboard* as it is the main point of contact for your fretting hand fingers.

Headstock: The uppermost part of the instrument, located at the end of the *neck*, above the *nut* and *fretboard*, where the *tuning posts* hold the strings in place. This is also the part where the manufacturer's name is displayed. Each model has its own distinctive shape.

Neck: Another major part of the bass connected to the body. This is where the *fretboard* lies. Necks can be carved out of the same piece of wood as the body (neck-through) or more commonly, be a separate piece altogether which is bolted on or glued to the body.

Nut: A grooved piece of bone, plastic, or metal through which the strings pass, separating the *fretboard* from the *headstock*. It is essentially fret number 0, and all frets are numbered relative to the nut.

Pickups: Basically a microphone for the electric bass guitar. They consist of a coil of copper wire wrapped around a magnet (one per string) and are typically housed inside a plastic or metal covering.

When a string is plucked, the magnetic field of the pickup is disturbed, creating magnetic flux which is then transmitted through a cable and converted into sound when it reaches an amplifier, producing a pitch. Pickups come in a variety of styles and are typically either single-coil or humbuckers, each with its own unique sound.

Strap Locks: Pegs upon which a strap can be fastened to facilitate playing while standing and to aid in adjusting the height of the guitar to the desired level.

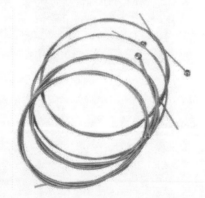

Strings: Arguably the most important part of the bass or any stringed instrument and the reason every other part of the instrument is there - because they are responsible for producing the sound! They are made of nylon or steel (and at one time, cat gut). A standard bass guitar has 4 of them, though up to 6-string variations of the bass exist. Technically they are not a permanent part of the instrument since they are replaceable and often break (if you can invent an unbreakable string, take my money).

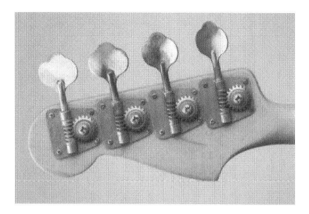

Tuning pegs: Used to raise or lower the desired pitch of each string by rotation, thereby tuning the strings. The pegs are attached to the headstock in 1 row of 4 or 2 rows of 2 (on a typical 4-string guitar).

Tone/Volume Controls: Also known as "pots," or potentiometers. They control the amount of output of certain parameters of sound. The volume pot obviously controls the volume, typically from 0-10 (though some guitars might go to 11!), 0 being no output and 10 being full output.

Tone controls add bass and subtract treble on one end and add treble and subtract bass on the other, with 0 being the most 'bassy' and 10 being the most 'trebly,' sort of like a mini wah-wah pedal.

How Bass Guitars Work

All instruments require some form of vibration to move the air around them and a produce a sound in a consistent and controllable frequency. The human voice uses vibrating vocal cords, the saxophone uses vibrating reeds, and stringed instruments like the violin, banjo, and bass guitar use, well, vibrating strings!

Plucking, or setting a string on the bass in motion, causes it to vibrate and produce a pitch. The more tense the string, the higher the pitch. The less tense the string, the lower the pitch (think about stretching and plucking a rubber band).

To change the pitch of a bass guitar string, we can turn the *tuning pegs* one way or the other to increase or decrease the tension, or we can alter the length of a string. Since the strings are of a set length, it is impossible to lengthen them, but it is possible to shorten them. To shorten the string, we press it down on the *frets* of the bass. The higher up the neck (toward the bridge) you fret a string, the higher the pitch, and vice versa.

So, pitch is achieved by shortening the strings on the bass. This is why mandolins and ukuleles sound higher-pitched than the bass.

Electric bass guitars use magnetic *pickups* to convert the vibration of the strings into an electrical signal which then passes through an *amplifier* and is turned into sound waves when it is output through a loudspeaker.

An **acoustic** bass guitar produces its sound acoustically. The vibrating strings transmit sound waves through the *body,* which resonate in the cavity of the instrument and out through the *sound hole(s),* just like the vibrations from your vocal cords resonate in the cavity of your mouth and exit through your lips.

THEORY NOTE: In western music, the *octave* is divided into 12 equal parts, meaning there are only 12 unique notes from which to choose (A A#/Bb B C C#/Db D D#/Eb E F F#/Gb G G#/Ab). This is called the *chromatic scale.* The shortest distance, or *interval,* between notes is called a *semitone* or 1/2 tone. On the guitar, a *semitone* is the distance between 2 adjacent frets (on the same string).

Tuning

Each string of the bass guitar is numbered from 1 to 4, with 1 being the skinniest and highest-pitched string and 4 being the thickest and lowest-pitched string. Standard tuning (the most common way to tune a bass) is as follows:

1st string = **G**

2nd string = **D**

3rd string = **A**

4th string = **E**

Typically, we express this from the lowest sounding string to the highest sounding string which looks like this:

E A D G

It is highly recommended that you purchase an electronic tuner or download a tuning app if you have a smartphone. There are many free options to choose from and it is an essential accessory.

PRO TIP: The first thing EVERY BASSIST, regardless of skill, should do before sitting down to practice, take a lesson, or play a gig is TUNE YOUR BASS!

If you don't have a tuner handy you can tune by ear, though this requires practice. If there is another in-tune instrument like a piano nearby (and you or a friend know the note names) you can try and match the pitch of each string to said instrument. So, start by tuning the 6th string by playing an E on the piano and using the tuning pegs on your guitar to make it match that pitch. Do this for every string.

Another popular method of tuning by ear is to use the **'5th fret trick.'** Assuming your 4th string is in tune, match each open string's pitch to the pitch of the 5th fret of the adjacent string below it in pitch.

Don't worry, it's easier done than said! To put it simply, the 5th fret of the low **E** string (4th string) should sound exactly the same as the open **A** string, as they are both A notes (if you play the 5th fret of the E string and the A doesn't match, you need to turn the tuning knob of the A string until it does). Apply the same to the other strings like so:

The 5th fret of the **A** string should sound like the open **D** string.

The 5th fret of the **D** string should sound like the open **G** string.

This diagram illustrates the **5th fret trick** to tuning:

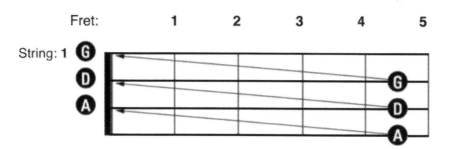

To sum it up, tuning is very important, and it is strongly advised that you get yourself a tuner.

Now that you know the important parts of the guitar and how the instrument works, let's start playing!

Chapter 3
First Notes

Topics covered:

- Learning to pluck open strings

- How to read *TAB*

- Fretting technique

- Technical warm-ups

- Posture and hand positioning

- Basic bass-lines on a common chord progression

Notes on the bass are sounded by plucking the strings. Pitches are raised or lowered by pressing down on the frets (a more detailed description can be found in Chapter 2). Each hand is tasked with a specific function when playing the bass. For right-handed players, the right hand plucks the strings and the left hand frets the notes, and vice versa for left-handed players. We will refer to these hands as the *plucking hand* and the *fretting hand*.

Plucking the strings with your fingers is called *fingerstyle* technique, and this is the most common way to pluck the bass. You can also use a *plectrum* or *pick* to pluck the strings, depending on the sound and style you are aiming for. Ideally, you should be able to play with both your fingers and a pick. Fingers on the *plucking hand* are labelled like this:

p = thumb

i = index

m = middle

a = ring

c = pinky

Fingers on the *fretting hand* are labeled like this:

T = thumb

1 = index

2 = middle

3 = ring

4 = pinky

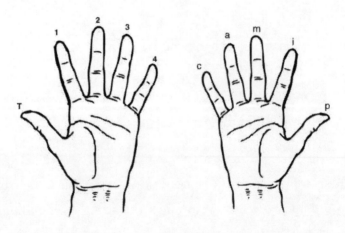

Labeled fretting hand and plucking hand fingers

Now let's learn about the notation system we'll be using throughout the book.

Tablature (TAB)

Stringed instrument players like guitarists, bassists, ukulele players, and even lutenists use a specialized graphic notation system called *tablature,* or TAB, which depicts the precise fingering and placement of notes on the fretboard (as opposed to specific musical pitches and rhythms like *standard notation*).

TAB uses 4 horizontal lines to represent the 4 strings of the bass guitar (there are also 5-string and 6-string bass versions) with the top line representing the highest (1st) pitched string, and the bottom line representing the lowest (4th) string. It is basically like looking at your fretboard upside down.

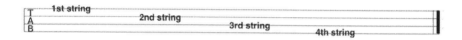

A blank measure of TAB, with strings labeled

Just like the words on this page, TAB is read from left to right, with notes on the right occurring later in time than notes on the left.

Notes in TAB are indicated by numbers placed on the lines. The numbers represent which fret to play, with 1 representing the 1st fret, 2 representing the 2nd fret, and so on. The number 0 represents the open strings, meaning you play the string without placing your finger on it.

You may also see music written in *standard notation,* which often appears above the TAB, but that is a subject for another day! For our purposes, we will be using the minimum required to get you started playing bass: TAB and fretboard diagrams.

For reference, Standard Notation looks like this.

With that out of the way, let's learn our first bit of music.

Playing Open Strings

Since bass is the lowest sounding instrument, we'll start from the bottom by using the lowest note on the bass, the open E-string.

<u>Example 1</u> is a simple exercise to get your *plucking hand* fingers moving, alternating between your *index* and *middle* fingers with your *fretting hand* free to do whatever it wants. It consists of 2 identical measures of 3 *quarter notes* followed by a *quarter note rest*. The double dotted thick bars that bookmark the example are *repeat* symbols.

Ex. 1

AUDIO EXAMPLE Track #2

It may not seem like much, but it's a start, and one note is often all you need for a memorable bass part. Let's take the same open-string concept as above but busy up the rhythm a bit.

<u>Example 2</u> uses both the open E-string and the open A-string, but this time we combine *quarter notes* and *eighth notes*. Note the plucking pattern and really try to lock in and keep a steady tempo throughout.

Ex. 2

AUDIO EXAMPLE Track #3

PRO TIP: When practicing your *plucking hand* technique, strive for even strokes with your *i* and *m* fingers, focusing on steady rhythm, volume, and tone. The goal is to make each finger stroke sound indistinguishable from the other. Bass is a physical instrument, so getting your fingers in shape should be a priority from the beginning! Now let's try to squeeze as much as we can out of our open strings and play something a little bit more musical.

Example 3 is based on a *12-bar blues* progression, something you may end up playing a lot in your bass guitar career. We will use the open A-string, D-string, and E-string in a basic *quarter note* rhythm. Our longest example yet, this little ditty is a whopping 12 measures long (as the name *12-bar blues* suggests), so try tackling it 4 measures at a time if you're having trouble.

Ex. 3

AUDIO EXAMPLE Track #4

Playing Fretted Notes

Playing exclusively open strings is fun, but there are so many more possibilities to explore! Let's move beyond the open position and put our *fretting hand* to work. Below are two images. The first shows proper fretting technique, with the finger pressed as close as possible to the *fret wire,* while the second shows improper fretting technique, with the finger in the middle of the fret.

PRO TIP: When learning to fret notes on the bass, it is quite common to encounter *buzzing* and/or *muting,* an unpleasant sound that should be avoided, unless the music calls for it, of course. Excluding physical defects in the instrument or strings (mechanical difficulties), there is a solution to eliminate *buzzing/muting!*

Problem: You're fretting the note wrong!

Solution: Fret the note right! This means you should be applying the correct amount of pressure so that the note rings out and placing your finger *right behind the fret wire*, NOT in the middle or back of the fret (read the section on posture).

In **Example 4** we still make use of the open A-string and open E-string but will introduce our 3rd and 1st *fretting hand* fingers to play the 3rd fret **G** note and 1st fret **F** note on the 4th string. Note the letters above each measure (Am, G, F, E). These are *chord symbols*, which we will address more thoroughly in the next chapter.

Ex. 4

AUDIO EXAMPLE Track #5

Pay close attention to the rhythm as the first half of each measure uses a *dotted quarter note* plus an *eighth note*. Attaching a dot to a rhythm adds half the value to a note. In this case, the dot is attached to a *quarter note*. Half of a *quarter note* is an *eighth note* and since a *quarter note* takes up one beat and an *eighth note* takes up half a beat, a *dotted quarter note* takes up one and a half beats.

Developing Simple Basslines

In the next few examples we will take an extremely common *chord progression* (known as the **I-V-vi-IV** progression) and develop several rhythmic variations to accompany it.

Example 5a uses only *whole notes* derived from the *roots* of each chord. By *root*, we mean the lowest note of each chord, which is where a chord gets its name. So, when you see chord symbols like those above each measure of the following examples, simply play the note that the chord is named after. For example: the root of a

D chord is **D**, the root of an **A chord** is **A**, and the root of a **Bm chord** is **B**. Simple, right? We will discuss this more later, but for now let's focus on playing! *Use your 1st finger to play the 2nd fret in bar 3 and your 2nd finger to play the 3rd fret in bar 4.*

Ex. 5a
AUDIO EXAMPLE Track #6

Example 5b takes the same notes from the previous example but adds a little bit of variation, making use of a repeated rhythmic figure of a *dotted half note* (which lasts for 3 beats) followed by a *quarter note*. Basically, you'll be playing notes on beats 1 and 4 throughout.

Ex. 5b
AUDIO EXAMPLE Track #7

Still using the same 4 notes from the previous 2 examples, **Example 5c** creates a bit more forward propulsion with a *syncopated* rhythm, which means that it makes use of accents on *offbeats*. In this case, there are rests on the *downbeats* of 2 and 4 and notes on the *upbeats*. Use alternating *i* and *m* strokes throughout.

Ex. 5c

AUDIO EXAMPLE Track #8

__Example 5d__ will be our final variation on the **I-V-vi-IV** progression. It uses a constant stream of *eighth notes* to create a steady, driving groove. Strive for even spacing between each note and a consistent tone and volume while alternating *i* and *m* fingers throughout.

Ex. 5d

AUDIO EXAMPLE Track #9

Let's Talk About Rhythm

Hopefully the previous examples in this chapter have your fingers moving and making actual music without getting bogged down with too many small details. Now we're going to take a step back and discuss **rhythm**. The bass is a key component of the *rhythm section* of most ensembles and a thorough knowledge of *rhythmic values* is integral to the study of bass guitar - or any musical instrument for that matter. RHYTHM IS KING.

Simply put, **rhythm** is how long a pitch is held. The dictionary defines it as *"the pattern of regular or irregular pulses caused in music by the occurrence of strong and weak melodic and harmonic beats."*

Without **rhythm**, music would be a chaotic mess of random noise. **Rhythm** exists all around us: a blinking traffic light, your heartbeat, the pistons in a car engine, the chirping of a bird, you get the picture!

Before we elaborate, let's define an important concept when discussing **rhythm**. The **beat** is the (typically steady) pulse, or a basic unit of time. Think of clapping your hands in time at a concert or snapping your fingers along to the radio. That is the **beat**. The dictionary defines it as *"the audible, visual, or mental marking of the metrical divisions of music."*

Rhythmic Values

When we change the appearance of a note in standard music notation, we change the rhythm. Notes are composed of three different elements: *note head, stem*, and *flag*.

Be advised: rhythmic values in this book are written above the TAB in standard notation.

The *note head* is the round part of the note. The *stem* is the vertical line attached to the right side of the *note head*. The *flag* is the curved line attached to the top or bottom of the *stem* (depending on its orientation).

Whole Note: This is the longest note used in standard notation. It looks like an open oval and lasts for 4 beats in 4/4 time. It is the equivalent of 4 **quarter notes**.

𝗢

Half Note: This note, as the name implies, is equivalent to exactly half the duration of a **whole note**. It looks like a **whole note** with a stem attached. It lasts for 2 beats in 4/4 time.

Quarter Note: This note is equivalent to a quarter of a **whole note** and half of a **half note**. It lasts for 1 beat in 4/4 time and looks like a filled in **half note** with a stem.

Eighth Note: This note results from splitting the **quarter note** in half and therefore lasts for ½ of a beat in 4/4 time. It looks like a quarter note with a flag attached. Groups of eighth notes are usually connected by **beams** in either twos or fours.

Sixteenth Note: This note has a duration of 1/16th of a whole note or ¼ of a quarter note. It looks like an **eighth note** with 2 flags and is typically beamed in groups of 4. It lasts ¼ of a beat.

You can theoretically subdivide each note until you are blue in the face. If you keep subdividing beats it will look something like this: one 16th note becomes two 32nd notes, one 32nd note becomes two 64th notes, one 64th note becomes two 128th notes, and so on.

All you need to do to indicate each successive note is add one more flag to the stem. Simple, right?

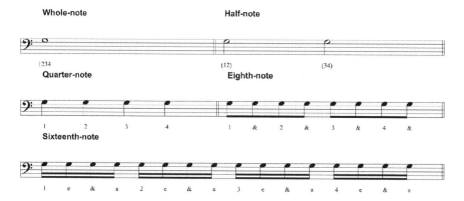

Warming Up

Before we close out the chapter we'll learn one of the most important things you can do for your technique and hand coordination: warm-up exercises. When you're starting out on an instrument as physical as the bass guitar it may be difficult to make the stretches required to properly fret the notes and your fingers may lack the physical strength and endurance to play for more than a few minutes.

The best way to develop this strength, endurance, and flexibility is with DAILY warm-up exercises. Seriously, you should start every single one of your practice sessions or performances by warming up. Any serious athlete stretches before a competition. Serious musicians are no different.

Example 6 is a tried, tested, and true chops-builder that activates all 4 fingers on your fretting hand, works your alternating plucking technique, and can cover the entire fretboard if you feel like it.

Ex. 6

AUDIO EXAMPLE Track #10

The basic idea of this exercise is this: *a)* Start on the 1st fret of the low E-string with your 1st finger, then play the 2nd fret with your 2nd finger, 3rd fret with your 3rd finger, and 4th fret with your 4th finger. *b)* Move to the adjacent string and repeat this pattern. *c)* Once you run out of strings, move your hand up 1 fret and then reverse the pattern, starting with your 4th finger and ending on your 1st finger, before moving to the adjacent string and repeating the pattern.

You can do this all the way up the neck until you run out of frets if you feel the need. Do this for a few minutes a day and you'll develop fingers of steel!

Eventually, you may get really good at this exercise and need a new challenge. Never fear, this exercise is almost endlessly variable and there are many **permutations** you can arrive at by simply changing the order of your fingers: 1-2-3-4, 1-3-4-2, 1-2-4-3, 2-4-

3-1, 4-2-3-1… the list goes on. You can also try skipping over a string here and there.

PRO TIP: Start by practicing these exercises SLOWLY and DELIBERATELY, focusing on proper technique, even tone, steady rhythm, and coordination between both hands. NEVER RUSH because you want to play faster.

SPEED is the byproduct of ACCURACY.

Chapter 4
Groove Theory

Topics covered:

- Musical alphabet

- Notes on the fretboard

- Chord and scale theory

- Building basslines with chord tones

- Major and minor chord shapes

Musical ABCs

The distances between musical notes are called "intervals," of which the smallest is called a *semitone* or *half-step*. On the bass, semitones are represented by the distance of one fret. For example, on the 1st string, the distance between the 1st fret and the 2nd fret is 1 *semitone*.

When you add 2 semitones together, you get what is called a *tone* or *whole step*. This distance is represented by the distance of two frets on the bass guitar, so the distance between the 1st string and 1st fret and the 1st string and 3rd fret is a *tone*.

The western musical alphabet consists of 7 letters (from A to G) and is made up of a sequence of *half steps* and *whole steps*. Each letter is separated by *whole steps* except for **B** and **C**, and **E** and **F**, which are a *half step* apart from each other. Think of these notes as inseparable friends that you always see together.

In the diagram below, one octave of the musical alphabet is laid out on top of a ruler, with each tick representing a half step:

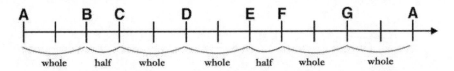

As long as you know what note you are on and remember the '**BC** and **EF** rule' you will easily be able to find any note on a given string. The above diagram can be replicated exactly on the 3rd string of the bass guitar (the A string) up to the 12th fret, with the first tick being represented by the open string and each subsequent tick being represented by the frets:

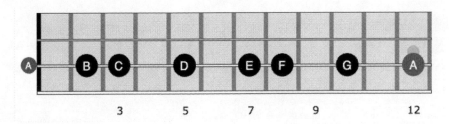

These notes (natural notes with no sharps or flats) are the equivalent of the white keys on the piano and comprise the C major/A minor scale. For additional practice, try playing these notes on all the strings of your bass.

For instance, if you were to play the 1st string, you'd have to first figure out what the open string note is (it's G). Knowing that the next note in our scale is A, we must then ask ourselves "is that a half step or a whole step away from G?" We know the answer is a whole step, which lets us know that we find the A on the 2nd fret. Proceed on this path until you have these relationships burned into your brain and fingers and you will be well on your way to understanding how the fretboard works!

Sharps (#) and flats (b)

The notes that reside between the natural notes are called *sharps* (indicated by a #) and *flats* (indicated by a *b*). To *sharpen* a note means to raise it by 1 semitone, so if you want to find a **C#** note, simply find a **C** note and raise the pitch by 1 semitone.

C = 8th fret, 1st string

+1 semitone

C# = 9th fret, 1st string

Flattening a note means to lower it by 1 semitone, so if you want to find an **Ab** note, simply find an **A** note and lower the pitch by 1 semitone.

A = 5th fret, 1st string

-1 semitone

Ab = 4th fret, 1st string

'Natural' Notes on Each String

In **Example 7**, let's look at exactly where to find the natural notes on the bass, up to the 12th fret. Beyond the 12th fret, the same pattern repeats itself until you run out of fretboard.

Ex. 7

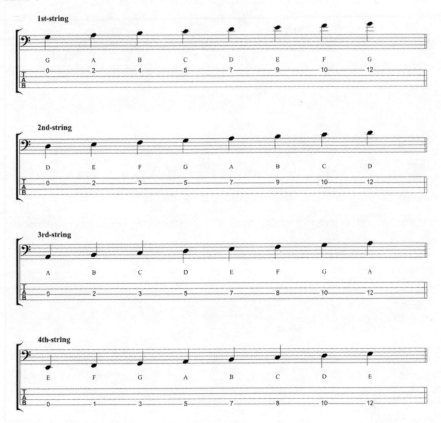

AUDIO EXAMPLE Track #11

PRO TIP: Learning the note names on the bass should be a priority FROM DAY ONE! Take a few minutes to quiz yourself each time you sit down to play. Can you find all the E notes on the bass guitar? Can you name all the notes on each string? "No" is not an acceptable answer to these questions.

Knowing the note names will enable you to name chords, identify scales and key signatures, communicate with other musicians, and develop a more universal understanding of music.

Moving Beyond the 'Root'

In the previous chapter you were introduced to the concept of creating simple basslines using only the *roots* of each chord of the progression. In this chapter we will go beyond that and give you more colors to paint with by introducing *chord tones*. First, let's learn exactly what a chord is and how to approach playing chords on the bass.

In western music, a **chord** is any *harmonic* set of 3 or more pitches sounded simultaneously. They are referred to as **arpeggios** when the pitches of a given chord are sounded separately, which is how they are typically heard on the bass (as the low frequency range of the bass tends to 'muddy up' multiple pitches played simultaneously).

The most basic and common types of chords are called **triads**, which are chords consisting of 3 notes stacked in the interval of a *third*. What does all of this mean?

Major Scale Formula

To understand how **triads** are constructed we need to understand how the **major scale** is constructed - the scale from which all chords are derived. A *scale* is simply a collection of ordered pitches. The **major scale** is a 7-note pitch collection (do-re-mi-fa-sol-la-ti) which is the basis of all western music. There are 12 **major scales**, one built off each note of the **chromatic scale**, and these 12 scales correspond to the 12 major *keys*. In the beginning of this chapter, we learned about *half steps* and *whole steps*.

The **major scale** is built from the following sequence of *whole steps* and *half steps:*

W-W-H-W-W-W-H

So, if we want to figure out the notes for say, a **C major scale,** we simply apply this formula to a **chromatic scale** starting on **C.** The beauty of this stepwise formula is that you can apply it to any note of the chromatic scale to derive any major scale. We will cover scale shapes on the bass a bit later, but for now let's look at how this applies to *chords*.

Chord Formulas

If we take our 7-note major scale formula and apply a number to each note, we get this in the key of **C:**

C = 1

D = 2

E = 3

F = 4

G = 5

A = 6

B = 7

Triads are made by stacking two *thirds*. A *third* interval is the distance between scale tone 1 and 3, 2 and 4, 3 and 5, etc. To build a **major triad**, we take notes **1** (or the root), **3,** and **5.** In the case of our **C major scale**, that gives us: **C E G.**

C is the **root, E** is the **3rd,** and **G** is the **5th.**

There are 4 types of **triads:** Major, Minor, Diminished, and Augmented. Here are their formulas as applied to the key of **C:**

Major = **1 3 5** (C E G)

Major = **1 b3 5** (C Eb G)

Diminished = **1 b3 b5** (C Eb Gb)

Augmented = **1 3 #5** (C E G#)

Each of these **triads** has a corresponding *chord symbol* for ease of reading. In the key of **C** they look like this:

C Major: **C**

C Minor: **Cm**

C Diminished: **Cdim** or **C°**

C Augmented: **Caug** or **C⁺**

Don't worry too much about this stuff; it takes time for these concepts to click. Let's get back to playing!

Using the Root and 5th

Now let's move beyond using just the root note in our basslines and throw in the 5th for some additional movement and color.

Root + 5th

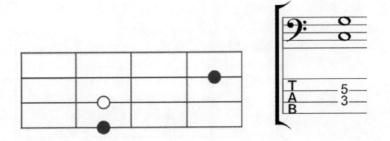

The diagram above is a graphic representation of the fretboard, with the 1st string as the top line and the 4th string as the bottom line. The frets are represented by vertical lines. The dots show you where to put your fingers. The *white dot* is the **root** and the *black dots* are the **5th**.

Example 8a is based on a classic 'boom-chick' or 'two-beat' rhythm used commonly in country, folk, and rockabilly music. It is based on a I-IV-V progression in the *key of* C (C = I, F = IV, and G = V) where you play the **root** of each chord on beats 1 and 3 and the **5th** on beats 2 and 4.

Ex. 8a

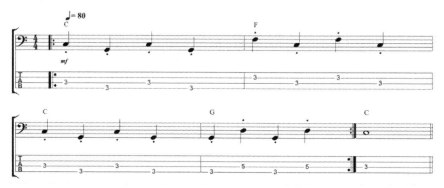

AUDIO EXAMPLE Track #12

Example 8b is a slight variation of the previous example where we replace the **5th** of the chord on the 4th beat of each bar with 2 eighth note *walk-ups* and *walk-downs* where we play 2 notes that lead into the **root** note on the 1st beat of each measure. This is a common trick used by bass players of all genres to give the music some forward momentum.

Ex. 8b

AUDIO EXAMPLE Track #13

For **Example 9**, we'll be injecting a little Brazillian flavor into our fingers, playing a *Bossa Nova* inspired groove in the *key of D* *minor.* The *fretting hand* retains the exact same shape throughout, fretting the **root** of each chord with the index finger and the **5th** with either the ring or pinky finger, depending on your preference. Notice the complex sounding chord symbols written above each measure (Dm9, Fmaj7, E7#9, Eb9)?

Don't be afraid. As a bass player, if you know the **root + 5th** shape, you can play most chords with just these two notes, unless it is indicated that the 5th is altered, but that is more advanced territory beyond the scope of this book.

Ex. 9

AUDIO EXAMPLE Track #14

Octaves

A similar shape to the **root + 5th** is the **root + octave**. An octave is double the frequency (higher-pitched) of a given root, or simply 8 notes away from your **root** in a major scale, which ends up having the exact same note name as your **root**. So, the octave of **C** is **C**, the octave of **F** is **F**, the octave of **G#** is **G#**... you get the point. Here's what the shape looks like:

Root + Octave

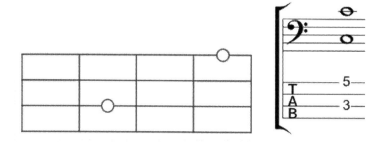

Many basslines have been created using not much more than the **octave** shape. You can hear it in funk, rock, and especially disco (Chic's Bernard Edwards was a master).

Disco is the inspiration for **Example 10**. This groove features a steady quarter note alternation between the **root** note and the **octave** along the 3rd and 1st string of the **Am** chord in bar 1 and the **Dm** chord in bar 3, which we will call our *target notes*. Bars 2 and 4 can be seen as transitional moments as we move from one *target note* to the next, and serve as *walk-ups* and *walk-downs,* similar to the ones featured in **Example 8b**.

Ex. 10

AUDIO EXAMPLE Track #15

<u>Example 11</u> takes the octave approach and applies a rhythm similar to the *Bossa Nova* pattern in **Example 9**, but in the context of a fairly straight forward rock-type groove.

AUDIO EXAMPLE Track #16

Major and Minor 3rds

We've come a long way since we first discussed the idea of **triads**. To recap, a triad is made up of 3 notes. In a major chord we use the notes **1** (or **root**), **3,** and **5**, derived from the 7-note major scale. In a minor chord, we use the notes **1, b3**, and **5**.

So far, we've played basslines using the **root** (and its higher **octave**) and the **5th**. Now we will incorporate the **3rd** into our playing to complete the holy trinity. Three is a magic number!

There are two types of **3rds:** *Major 3rds* or **M3** for short, and *Minor 3rds* or **m3**.

Here's how they look on the fretboard:

Root + M3

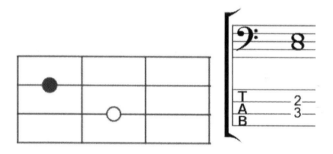

Root + m3

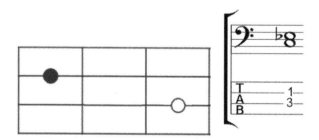

Example 12 takes the same chord sequence as the bassline we developed in Chapter 4 and adds a splash of much needed color by using **root + 3rd** ideas. As a general rule, use a major 3rd (**M3**) on major chords and a minor 3rd (**m3**) on minor chords. There are 3 major chords in this example (D, A, and G) and 1 minor chord (Bm).

Ex. 12

AUDIO EXAMPLE Track #17

PRO TIP: To get the most bang for your buck from this book, try to go back to some of the previous examples and apply the knowledge you've gleaned up to this point. For instance, try to add major or minor 3rds, 5ths, or octaves to the basslines in Chapter 4. Find the chords to a simple song you like and try to figure out the notes you need to play. All these things we are learning MUST BE APPLIED to real music. Isn't that why you came here?

Major and Minor Triads

At long last we have arrived. Here's what the **Major triad** (**root, 3rd,** and **5th**) and the **minor triad** look like on the bass guitar:

Major Triad

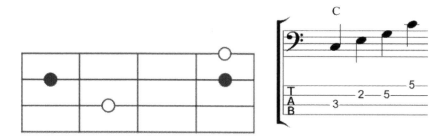

Minor Triad

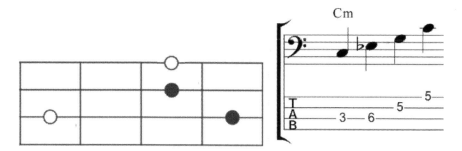

Example 13 is a laid back, reggae-inspired groove that makes use of all the notes of each **triad** over a common **I-vi-ii-V** (G, Em, Am, D) chord progression. Before tackling the example as written, make sure to slowly practice the triad for each chord on its own. It is important to break things up into bite-sized chunks.

AUDIO EXAMPLE Track #17

To close out the chapter, here's a *12-bar blues* boogie that's a bit more advanced than the 12-bar blues we played in **example 3**.

Example 14 uses all major chords based on the standard blues form in the key of A major. We play a steady **root-3rd-5th-3rd** triad sequence over each chord of the tune.

If you compare it to our simple, root-note-only blues groove from Chapter 4, it demonstrates just how much momentum and sense of movement you can create by *arpeggiating* chord tones, which means playing each note of a given chord one-by-one. It's much more interesting than simply playing the root!

AUDIO EXAMPLE Track #18

Unlock Your Musical Potential: Get 30% Off the Next Step in Your Instrumental Journey

As a token of appreciation for your dedication, we're excited to offer you an **exclusive 30% discount** on your next product when you sign up below with your email address.

Click the link below:
https://bit.ly/40NikR2
OR
Use the QR Code:

Unlocking your musical potential is easier with ongoing guidance and support. Join our community of passionate musicians to elevate your skills and stay updated with the latest tips and tricks.

By signing up, you'll also receive our periodic newsletter with additional insights and resources to enhance your musical journey.

Your privacy is important to us. We won't spam you, and you can unsubscribe anytime.

Don't miss out on this opportunity to continue your musical journey with this special discount. Sign up now, and let's embark on this musical adventure together! 🎼